BLACK GIRLS DON'T CRY

UNVEILING OUR PAIN AND UNLEASHING HOPE

*Stephen,
You ARE the
MAN of MY
DREAMS!*

ANGELICA LEIGH

Cover Design by Karen D. Harris/-ize on design

To My Daughters: Remember to put all your trust in God as you take your journey into woman-hood. Never forget your worth is more precious than rubies.

Nya- let your gift of creativity lead you into your purpose.

Trinity- embrace the big heart God has given you, and follow your dreams without ceasing.

ACKNOWLEDGEMENTS

To my mommy, Martha, you've been such a strong force in my life. You've shown me how to be a woman of God, and provided me with the tools I needed to stand on my own two feet. You've sacrificed so much for us and I want to say thank you for all that you've done and STILL continue to do.

To my daddy, Tyrone, thank you for planting the seed of "optimism" in me. You've always encouraged us to be entrepreneurs, and not to settle for anything less than the best. Your determined and friendly, easy-going spirit has poured onto me, and without you I wouldn't have been able to dream as big as I do!

Patricia, your support and encouragement was much appreciated. Alyse, your feedback was invaluable. Jan and Josh, thank you for always believing in me, and encouraging me to not give up.

Special thanks to everyone who contributed to the completion of this book: Karen Harris, thank you for the awesome cover! All the long hours you put into this project editing and guidance throughout this entire process is greatly appreciated. Lee Harris, thank you for capturing such an amazing portrait of me.

To Tyrone and Jovon thank you for all your support!

To my best friend, Brad, thank you for unselfishly giving me time to write this book. You've been in my corner cheering me on, and comforted me as I revealed some of my deepest scars. You were right there to lift my spirits on days when I felt like just giving up. Thank you for being the husband I've always dreamed of.

TABLE OF CONTENTS

ABOUT THE TITLE

When you think of an African American woman what are some traits that come to mind? For me, I think of strength, fortitude, and sacrifice. Many will come up with different answers depending on the environment you grew up in and the women around you. I remember watching my mom when I was younger. As a single parent, she worked, cooked, cleaned and kept all three of her children in order.

She seemed to have handled everything effortlessly. I never heard her complain about having to do everything on her own. Even when things were tight financially, she held it all together with a smile. I'm sure at times she wanted to just break down and cry, but she would never do that in front of us. As African-American women, we are often looked to as the glue that holds everything together. We're the backbone for our husbands and the comfort for our children.

Our hurts, pains and struggles are often overlooked. We lose ourselves in our families, work and other responsibilities. Our "issues" often take the backseat so that we can be a help to others in need. Black Girls Don't Cry uncovers some of those hurts and insecurities we all have felt at some point. This is my personal journey of battling with low self-esteem and purpose. I pray it uplifts and touches those who may be going through a storm of their own.

DAY DREAMS

Bradley and I were packing boxes preparing to move. It had been a long time coming, but we were finally moving into our very own house. Renting had become a pain. So being able to own a home was a blessing. We had the majority of things loaded in the truck. I walked through the house to make sure we weren't leaving anything behind. I looked in the closet and checked the shelves. When I reached the top shelf I felt something that had been pushed against the wall. I couldn't quite figure out what it was, so I grabbed a stool to get a better grip.

To my amazement it was my old journal I'd started keeping about a year ago. I used to write about past experiences, and I found that it helped me release pain I'd been carrying around with me. I was so excited I'd found my journal because it contained very personal memories. It appeared to have a few pages missing, but I didn't mind. I was relieved we hadn't left it behind. I found a cozy spot in a corner on the floor and began to read.

This Journal Belongs To:

Angelica

JANUARY 6
Memory Lane

My earliest memory takes me back to when I was about five or six. I sat in the kitchen while my mother put up Christmas decorations. Sounds of the Temptations' Christmas album played in the background while she sang in between telling my brothers to go get more boxes from the basement.

I remember being alone in the kitchen and for some reason I thought I could make bubbles come out my mouth, so I went for the dish soap. It tasted awful! The next thing I recall is my mom frantic on the phone with poison control. I thought to myself "I'm going to die!" Luckily, all I needed was a little milk, and a good night's rest.

As a young girl I remember questioning everything. I always wanted an explanation as to why I was in trouble, and if anyone of you grew up with "old fashioned" parents you know this was a no-no. Questions like, "Why do we call grass, grass?" and "Why is a chair a chair?" Sometimes I would have these moments of disbelief and amazement saying to myself, "I'm really here, me Angelica Wilson is on the earth living, breathing, talking and thinking!"

From the outside looking in, many would say I had a pretty normal childhood. They didn't know how I struggled with my self-esteem or how I prayed and cried at night wishing my parents would get back together. I have no memories of my dad ever living with us, but I always felt there was a piece to my puzzle that was missing.

JANUARY 10
Waiting

As a young girl I would count down the days until it was time to go over to my dad's house. It was normally a nice getaway from my mother's strict rules. It was Friday, my brothers and I sat in the kitchen waiting for our dad to pick us up. We were so excited about what we might do that weekend. He would always take us somewhere fun whether it was the park, skating, bowling etc. In my mind my dad was the coolest.

An hour had past without noticing and still no dad. My mom began to get that familiar look on her face as if he wasn't coming. I figured he was probably running late, but he'd definitely be here for sure.

Two hours later, no call, and still no dad. It was about 9pm when my mom told us to take our bags upstairs because he wasn't coming. I looked at my brothers and I could see their hurt. I couldn't understand why he hadn't shown up or called.

The lonely feeling I felt in my heart is hard to forget. I went to my room and cried. I knew my dad loved us, but as I kid I felt like we weren't important enough to him. I was so angry because it was so unfair. What did I do to deserve this? I felt so unwanted. We were the only kids on our block whose parents were divorced. This mere fact made me sick.

JANUARY 15
My Daddy Told Me I Was Beautiful

One of my favorite shows growing up was Full House. I loved the closeness of their family. I related to Stephanie the most. In my eyes she was tough and pretty. She seemed to have everything I'd always wanted. I could sit and watch that show for hours at a time. Unknowingly, I believe this show began to shape my definition of beauty. I defined beauty as having long straight hair, being light skinned and slender. When I looked in the mirror I didn't see any of those things. I began to pick myself apart everyday. I was too skinny, too dark, with big lips and nappy hair! I hated the way I looked, and getting teased by other kids didn't help.

I wanted to be "that" girl. The one everyone thought was smart, funny and attractive. I remember seeing pictures *of myself and wanting to rip them off the wall. I used to think if I was white my life would be so much better. I know that's a terrible feeling to have, but I wished for it often. Although my father always told me I was beautiful, I figured he just didn't know what real beauty was.*

FEBRUARY 16
Flat As a Wall

"Your chest is so flat, it looks like a brick wall with graffiti on it," my neighbor yelled. Laughter immediately filled the room. I stood there hurt with tears filling my eyes as I struggled to keep from crying. I kept telling myself "Don't let them see you cry." I was wearing my favorite t-shirt with "Tweety Bird" printed on the front. I was always teased for not having curves like other girls. Although I was only in the fifth grade, the kids in my neighborhood were older than me and had already started developing. I thought I was supposed to have boobs too. That night I went home and stood in front of the mirror. I was so upset that God had made me this way. I began to feel unwanted and ugly. I cried myself to sleep that night and prayed I would wake up in a new body. I learned to hide my growing insecurities with slick comebacks and jokes. I guess you can say I adapted to being ugly and flawed.

My reading was interrupted by a loud noise at the door. I ran to see what it was. Josh and Brad had dropped my large mirror right outside the door. I scolded them both and told them to be careful with my things. I went back in the bedroom and sat for a moment. I began to reflect on my childhood. All the memories came flooding back into my mind. At that moment I could recall just how crippling my pain and insecurities had been.

I beat myself up for years because I thought I was missing something. I wish someone would have told me "You're only 11, you don't need any boobs!" It's funny that even at such a young age we can allow our peers' opinions of us to shape how we feel about ourselves. I never felt comfortable being in my own skin.

Often times we don't realize how important self-esteem really is. For those of you who struggle with similar issues, we don't know where or how the insecurities started. I'm sure they're many factors that contributed to my issues, but I believe that what we watch on TV, especially as children, plays an impact on how we view ourselves. There was a study conducted by Indiana University that found that TV viewing can actually negatively alter a child's self-esteem. They discovered that black children and white girls have lower perceptions of themselves after watching television.

We must make an effort to guard our minds and the things we expose ourselves to. Self-esteem is your foundation. If you start on shaky ground chances are you won't be able to withstand the trials of life. You'll be easily tricked and taken advantage of. The soundest way to build or rebuild your self-esteem is to discover who you are in Christ. Once you establish your ground in Christ you'll have a foundation that no man can shake!

I noticed on several pages I'd written motivational scriptures:

CONFIDENCE:

KNOWING AND BEING COMFORTABLE WITH WHO YOU ARE. BEING SECURE WITH YOUR GIFTS AND KNOWING THAT GOD HAS PLACED EVERYTHING WITHIN YOU THAT YOU NEED TO SUCCEED.

"BUT AS MANY AS RECEIVED HIM, TO THEM GAVE HE POWER..."
JOHN 1:12

MARCH 24
The Round Table

I sat at a round table with other students who had been selected from various middles schools to participate in a focus group. I can't quite remember what we were discussing, but I will never forget the feeling of inferiority that I felt that day. I was the only black girl in the group. There were other black kids there, but I ended up being the only one in my group. I remember two of the students in particular attended private school. Their uniforms looked extra clean and crisp, and they talked as if their parents were wealthy politicians. I began to sink in my chair as the negative thoughts filled my mind, "I don't want to say the wrong thing and sound stupid, what if they laugh at me?" I felt little and as worthless as a ball of lint sitting next to them. I couldn't wait until this was over.

My insecurities turned into anger as I said to myself "They think they're better than me." I was jealous of their confidence. They spoke and carried themselves well, and because I had so many insecurities bottled up, I figured I could never be as perfect as they were. They possessed something that I longed for, but I'd set a barrier in my mind that having confidence "like that" was out of my grasp.

I spent most of life feeling inferior to others. I noticed that I was giving them more esteem than I gave myself. I noticed between my personal trials and the enemy telling me lies, I believed that I was inadequate. Nothing else had been able to encourage me besides the word of God. I picked up the bible and came across a scripture, "The kingdom of God is within you." Luke 17:21. This little sentence was full of so much power. Everything I needed to succeed and overcome my issues could be done through Christ.

I don't know why it's so easy for us to believe that we can't do something vs. knowing we can. I guess when the odds are stacked up against us it's hard to defeat those odds. The key word in that statement is "hard" not impossible.

I hear about different success stories from time to time. One that sticks out in my mind is about Charles Darrow, an unemployed salesman. He spent years working dead end jobs to support his family. In the little spare time that he had, he would draw the streets of Atlantic City on his kitchen table cloth. He eventually made a game of it. Soon many friends would come over to play and requested that he make them copies to take home. He began selling the game to department stores.

When the demand for the game rose, he tried selling his idea to a game manufacturer called Parker Bros. They immediately dismissed his idea saying it contained too many errors. Charles continued to sell his game at department stores and hired additional help.

Eventually, Parker Bros took another look at the game and offered to buy it and pay Darrow the royalties, which made him a millionaire. Charles Darrow is the inventor of the well known family board game, "Monopoly".

I wondered how he was able to overcome. What I discovered is that he didn't give up, and he didn't believe the lies of fear, inadequacy and defeat. Somehow he trained his mind to actually believe that he could achieve anything he set out to do. Crazy right? The bible tells us that, "The things, which are impossible with men, are possible with God." Luke 18:27.

"People are quite remarkable when they begin thinking they can do things. All of man's greatest accomplishments have come after they've learned this little secret."
---Norman Vincent Peale

ASSERTIVENESS:

*KNOWING WHAT YOU WANT OUT OF
LIFE AND REFUSING TO STOP UNTIL YOU
GET IT. KNOW FOR CERTAIN YOU CAN
DO ANYTHING YOU PUT YOUR MIND
TO. ANYTHING IS POSSIBLE, EVEN WHAT
OTHERS BELIEVE TO BE IMPOSSIBLE.
THINK WITHOUT LIMITS! ASK FOR
WHAT YOU WANT WITH THE SAME
ASSURANCE AS IF YOU WERE GETTING
SOMETHING BACK THAT WAS STOLEN
FROM YOU!*

*"ASK, AND IT SHALL BE GIVEN YO; SEEK
AND YE SHALL FIND; KNOCK, AND IT
SHALL BE OPENED UNTO YOU"
MATTHEW 7:7*

APRIL 14
The Not So Blended Family

I remember going to my dad's in-laws' house. I felt dirty and ugly around them. Sometimes I felt like they didn't want me drinking out of their glasses. Talk about being the pink elephant in the room. My brothers and I were the only black kids there. It was one the most uncomfortable feelings. They were always nice and polite, but I often wondered what they really thought about us. I was often afraid to talk around them, so I was extra careful about how I said each word. I didn't want to sound "uneducated". I thought I had to prove myself. I felt so very small.

Where did these feelings of inferiority come from? No one ever told me I was less than or beneath. Why wasn't I comfortable? Somewhere along the road, I developed an inferiority complex.

I began to get nervous around people white and black. I immediately felt inadequate in almost every situation. My foundation had been set. Unfortunately mine was built with the quicksand of low self-esteem, insecurities and inadequacy. This opened the door for mistreatment, degradation and abuse.

These feelings stayed with me throughout my childhood and into early adulthood. I often had trouble speaking up. It was as if I'd created a jail for myself in my mind.

RELEASE ME:
A Message from the Powerful Voice Within

Release me to be happy and secure with
myself,
Allow me to feel beautiful inside and out,
Stop doubting me every time I'm faced
with a challenge,
Put away the crippling fear that lingers
throughout my mind,
I am one of a kind and should not be
compared to anyone else,
Stop allowing the opinions of others to
determine the next step I take,
Allow me to shine, to step out and be
noticed!
Insecurities, inferiority, fear, depression
and worthlessness....YOU HAVE NO
PLACE HERE ANY LONGER!
I'm ready to discover my talents,
And my reasons for being here,
I'm ready to walk with confidence,
And to speak without fear,
The time has come that I be FREED!
Now I demand for you to RELEASE ME!!!

AWARENESS:

IT'S SO IMPORTANT TO KNOW WHAT'S
GOING ON AROUND YOU. BE OPEN
AND AWARE OF WHEN GOD IS
SPEAKING AND DIRECTING YOU.

"INCLINE YOUR EAR, AND COME UNTO
ME: HEAR, AND YOUR SOUL SHALL LIVE"
ISAIAH 55:3

APRIL 17
Alone

My mother and I hadn't been getting along for awhile. It seems like our relationship went downhill when I started dating my new boyfriend. I don't remember what started this particular argument, but she put me on punishment. I was about 16 at the time so I "thought" I was grown. I began packing a bag of clothes and opened my window.

I threw the bag out first to gauge the distance down. I told myself there was no turning back now, and then I jumped. I hit the ground harder than I thought because it took a moment for me to get up and realize where I was. I grabbed my bag and began to walk. I was scared and alone. It was about 11pm and I had no idea where I would go. I just knew I couldn't stay with my mom anymore.

My life seemed to be getting so out of control. I felt like no one understood me, or cared about anything I was going through. Looking back I know it was nothing but the grace of God that kept me from harm that night.

There were many nights I would just cry myself to sleep. The pain of loneliness was so strong it was overwhelming. At your lowest point when you feel like no one understands and you're all alone, just remember, God knows and He cares. He is waiting for us to put our trust in Him, and let go of all our problems, hurts and pains.

MAY 1
As foul as spit

I sat in the car listening to my boyfriend yell and scream. The next thing I can remember is him turning to me with an evil look in his eyes as he spit in my face. It landed right in the corner of my eye. At that moment my natural reaction was to lash out and punch him in the face, but I decided not to in fear of what he might do in return. I was so angry and disgusted that I couldn't speak. I sat there in disbelief as tears filled my eyes. The whole time his cousin sat in the backseat watching quietly. I was about 18, and I have never been as humiliated in my life as I was that day. How could he do this to me? Am I really this worthless? My heart began hurting so bad. I snapped out of the trance and looked at him. He began yelling and told me to get out of his car. I got out, slammed the door and began walking home. That felt like the longest walk ever.

MAY 2
The Secret

I sat in the bathroom as my world seemed to spin. Everyone had such high hopes for me. I wasn't supposed to make any mistakes. I was the "good girl". How could I be pregnant? Why wasn't I more careful? What would my parents say? All my dreams started to crumble before my eyes.

I was so scared. How could I overcome this? I felt like such a failure and disgrace. Here I was 19, unmarried and pregnant. Where would we live? How would I support my family? All these thoughts flooded my mind. Although I had many doubtful feelings, there was a small piece of optimism within me. I fed on that feeling and decided I would make it through this.

The journey would be difficult, but quitting now wasn't an option. I would give my all to better myself, and provide the best life possible for my baby.

As afraid as I was, I took a deep breath looked in the mirror then I took the first step towards my future in motherhood. It took me months to finally break the news to my mother. I was so afraid of disappointing her. I remember calling her crying, "Mom I'm pregnant." To my amazement she responded, "I already knew because the doctor called to schedule your prenatal appointment." All this time I "thought" I was keeping this big secret, but she was just waiting for me to tell her. I guess my secret wasn't a "secret" after all.

MAY 8
Burn

I was about eight months pregnant with my daughter. My boyfriend had started on another one of his anger rants. I can't remember why he was so angry. He stood up over me with a bottle of rubbing alcohol in his hands. I looked into his eyes and saw nothing but darkness. He filled the cap of the bottle with alcohol, lit it with a lighter and threw it on me. He said he was going to set me on fire! I quickly tried to jump away from the burning alcohol as it hit my jeans. Luckily the flames blew out. I couldn't believe he would do this. Not only was he putting me in danger but our unborn child too. I left that night and stayed with my mom. How could someone be so evil? He had no regard for anyone, not even us.

DISCERNMENT:

KNOW HOW TO EVALUATE YOUR SITUATION AND MAKE THE BEST DECISION POSSIBLE. DEVELOP TRUST AND FAITH IN GOD THAT HE WILL GUIDE YOU THE RIGHT WAY.

"TRUST IN THE LORD WITH ALL THINE HEART AND LEAN NOT UNTO THINE OWN UNDERSTANDING"
PROVERBS 3:5

JUNE 28
Oil & Water Don't Mix

I'd just put the finishing touches to the pasta salad I had made for my boyfriend to take with him to a card party. He came in the kitchen and asked for my keys. I told him I would be dropping him off because I didn't want to be stuck at home all day. He was not too happy with this. I guess he had other plans which included taking my car. The next thing I knew a small disagreement had escalated into a full blown yelling match.

He walked to the dresser, grabbed the baby oil and began to squirt it all over me. Within moments I was dripping from my hair and face down to my shirt with oil. I thought to myself "He's lost his mind." With all that he wasn't done. He punched me in the stomach.

Then walked to the kitchen and put a cup of hot water in the microwave. He had threatened to burn me with it. I was terrified so I grabbed my cell phone and called the police.

By the time they arrived I was in tears. He had fabricated a lie that he was making hot chocolate in spite of it being the middle of the summer. After they made him leave I sat there once again in disbelief. I turned and looked at my two month old daughter sitting in her swing. She had been sitting there quietly throughout the entire episode. I knew I couldn't keep doing this. I didn't want her growing up in a dysfunctional environment. I felt like my life was ruined because I never wanted to raise a child on my own.

One of the officers stayed back to talk to me. I know I had to have looked pathetic sitting there with my hair full of oil as I cried uncontrollably. He asked me why I would stay with someone who treats me that way. I remember telling him I thought he would change. He then told me something that changed my perspective, "If he hasn't changed by now, he's not going to." He was right! He had never actually "hit" me before until now.

I shared with him some of the things I'd been through with my boyfriend and how he called me fat, ugly and said that nobody would want me because I had a baby. He almost laughed out as I went on. The officer snapped me back into reality. He said "You need to tune into you."

I had been so torn up inside believing all the lies he had told me. I allowed him to give and take away my confidence as he pleased. My life revolved around our relationship and without it

I felt I was nothing. I told the officer I didn't want to be alone. He said, "If you aren't comfortable with being alone with you, how can you expect anyone else to be happy with you?" He was right! I needed to "Tune into me".

After being in an abusive relationship I told myself I would take some time out to heal, but I longed to be with someone who truly loved me. I wanted the perfect family that I'd always dreamed of. I cried myself to sleep many nights because I felt like such a failure. I remember wishing I had listened to my family and friends when they would tell me he was no good. My self-esteem was pretty low when I met him and he did a great job of taking advantage of this fact.

No one ever knew just how much pain I was in. I became very good at making people think my life was perfect, when deep down I felt terrible. I never wanted anyone to worry or feel sorry for me. I was actually doing more damage to myself by holding it all in. I became confused about everything in life. My goals and dreams that were once clear became distant and unattainable. I found myself in a very low place. I'd been beat down emotionally to the point I believed now, that I really was worthless.

I stopped reading for a moment and rested my head up against the wall. I'd almost forgotten about the horrible situations I'd been in. Looking back I question what made me continue to go back to him time after time.

What I'm discovering is that I always thought he would change, and I never wanted to give up on him too soon. I just wanted things to be fun again, like they were when we first met.

Having that pattern of thinking can be very dangerous. Year after year things would get worse. The things he had once said he wouldn't do, he did.

JULY 29
A Family Reunion

I was about 20 when I attended my first family reunion, in Cincinnati, OH. We traveled about four hours anxiously waiting to meet our distant relatives. This was the first time my daughter and I had traveled anywhere together. I was a little sad that my six year relationship went sour, but life without the drama was good. We arrived safely and checked into the hotel.

The first event for the day was a walk through the National Underground Railroad Museum. It was nice learning about black history while getting to know family. As we strolled around the gift shop a man walked up to us. I remember seeing him in our group when we first arrived, but I wasn't sure who he was.

He smiled at me and said, "How old are you?" I told him I was twenty. He said, "Wow, you had a baby at 20? You're so young." I told him I actually had her when I was 19. He sarcastically responded "Wow that's impressive." He walked away right after the comment. I stood there very angry. This man didn't know anything about my past or what I'd been through. How dare he say something like that? My heart began hurting as the feelings of worthless filled my being.

Here I was trying to move on from my mistakes, and yet my "family" was right there to remind me that I was a failure. I wanted to go back to the hotel and cry. This happened many years ago, but I can still remember like it was yesterday. I wanted to prove him wrong so badly. I wanted to go to him and explain that I may have made a mistake, but I WILL overcome!

AUGUST 1
Speak

My spirit was screaming from within me. I wanted so badly to tell him to stop, but my lips just wouldn't form the words. What was wrong with me? Why couldn't I just tell him I didn't want to have sex? I didn't owe him anything." Tell him to stop! Tell him to stop!" my conscience cried out inside. Still no words would come out my mouth. So I laid there waiting for it to be over. A few minutes seemed to have lasted for hours. I wanted to cry. Here I was setting my morals aside as I allowed him take a piece of me.

The words began to get blurry as my eyes filled with tears. I remembered the pain I used to feel at times when I had sex. I would get so angry and full of guilt because I didn't speak up.

My self-esteem issues had gotten so bad that I wanted to be in a relationship at almost any cost. I would settle for men I knew didn't deserve me. I found myself going in and out of relationships giving more than what I was receiving. I always had a desire to "live right", a life that was acceptable and pleasing to Christ, but I didn't want to risk losing the relationship and being alone.

The irony in this is that if I would've chosen to do right and trust God, I would've gained the greatest relationship of all, with a guarantee that He would never leave my side.

AUGUST 12
Breathe

I lied back in the chair as the technician squirted warm gel on my belly. She moved the scope around my stomach until the embryo came into view. Tears began to roll down the side of my cheeks. Could I really go through with this? He sat by my side advising me not to look at the screen.

How bad had my situation gotten? I had become convinced that I would not have made it if I had another baby. The thoughts and opinions of what others might say about me were crippling. I didn't want anyone to think I was a failure. I didn't want to be a "disappointment". I was about four weeks pregnant when I got an abortion. I still carry around heaviness in my heart that I haven't been able to release. I felt like such a terrible person for what I had done.

Everyone deserves a chance to live, and I let fear of failure and others opinions stop a life that God had created. I prayed and cried many nights asking God for forgiveness. I vowed to NEVER allow my present situation or judgments of others determine my future.

Living with the pain of regret is very difficult. We all have some type of "should've, could've, would haves" in life. The key thing to remember is that it is in the past. As far as I know, no one has the ability to go back in time and change their past. So why waste time thinking about what you would have done differently. Acknowledge your mistakes, learn from them and move on. At times we get stuck at the "acknowledging" step we forget about moving forward.

The beauty of God's mercy is that when we confess our sins and ask for forgiveness, he wipes our slate clean. Not only does he forgive us, but he erases it from his memory. He will no longer hold us accountable for our mistakes. If only we could let go of our own guilt, regrets and failures the way God does. We aren't defined by our past; instead we're defined by what we can be through Christ!

The bible tells us to, "Confess your faults one to another, and pray one for another that ye be healed. The effectual fervent prayer of a righteous man availeth much." James 5:16

AUGUST 16
The Struggle

I remember going through rough times raising my daughter alone. There were times when I didn't know where her next pack of diapers would come from, or if I had enough gas to make it to work. I felt like I'd dug myself in a deep hole that I didn't know how to get out of. Those first few years seems to have gone by fast. Looking back my memories are a little fuzzy. I remember sleeping a lot to escape the nightmare I was living.

I found myself broken into pieces that had been scattered throughout unfulfilling jobs, thrown away by undeserving partners, and crushed by unattained dreams. I was at one of the lowest points in my life and I knew the only one who could put me back together was God.

I was tired of living below my abilities, tired of accepting less than what I deserved. At that moment I decided to stop feeling sorry for myself. I refused to let my life slip away without discovering my purpose and fulfilling it.

I began to share my experiences with others and I found that helped me heal. I no longer was ashamed of my past. I heard a life coach named Tracy Washington once say, "Your mess is your ministry!" You're not truly delivered from a situation until you're able to speak freely about it. I decided not to let my experiences be in vain. Instead I'd use it to help someone who may be going through similar problems.

"But as for you, you meant evil against me; but God meant it for good, in order to bring it about as it is this day, to save many people alive" Genesis 50:20

PERSERVERANCE:

NEVER GIVE UP ON YOURSELF. YOUR DREAMS AND ASPERATIONS ARE WORTH FIGHTING FOR!

"AND LET US NOT GROW WEARY WHILE DOING GOOD, FOR IN DUE SEASON WE SHALL REAP IF WE FAINT NOT"
GALATIANS 6:9

SEPTEMBER 21
Purpose

I was driving home from work one day and I called my mother. We talked awhile like we always did and I asked her a question, "What are your dreams? You know, what are you passionate about?" She paused for moment and responded "I don't have any." I fought with her a moment and then she finally said, "I like to design and decorate things." Then I asked her had she ever thought of owning her own business. She said, "No, I never thought it was possible. I never thought as big as you." At that moment her statement really touched me. Growing up she never thought she could do anything more besides getting a nine to five job. She said she was never as outgoing as I was.

As outgoing as she may have thought I was, I too often felt defeated. I always felt deep down that I was destined for something great, but I never actually believed it. I've struggled for years with encouraging myself and following my dreams. That has been by far one of the hardest things I've had to do.

Job after job I would become more and more dissatisfied with my situation. I didn't want my life to wisp away without figuring out my reason for being here. Feeling "purposeless" is very draining and at times I would feel like a robot just going through the motions.

I remember lying in the bed feeling miserable and defeated, like I had ruined my entire life. My husband asked what's wrong. I told him that I hated my job, and that just wanted to figure out my purpose.

He asked me a simple question that still to this day has changed my outlook on the whole "finding your purpose" goal. He asked, "If I wake up everyday, and ask God for direction so that I can obey Him, and I do just that, then how can I miss my purpose obeying God?" Although it may not "feel" like you're on the right path, trust that God has you where you're supposed to be. The obstacles we go through are apart of the journey into our purpose, and I've decided to enjoy the ride!

OCTOBER 31
Baggage Theory

There I was standing with all my bags, all my issues, insecurities and feelings of inadequacy. They were weighing me down to the point I could hardly take another step. Thoughts of suicide, depression, giving up on life itself were all around me. I knew I could either let my baggage continue to weigh me down, or I could drop the fear, insecurities and self-doubt and let today be the first day of a new beginning. I choose to drop the baggage and take the first step to recovery and that was LOVING ME!

It took me many years to be freed from the torment of low self-esteem, depression, and worthlessness. I began feeling insecure at a very young age.

It seems like I had been faced with issues early on before I was even able to get a good grasp of my worth and who I was. I wished I had someone I could talk to about how I was feeling, someone who wouldn't judge me, and would help me feel better about myself. The funny thing is that even if I had someone to talk to, I was too afraid of telling anyone how I really felt. I feared what they might think of me. Although I hid it well, the pain I felt inside everyday reminded me it was real.

DECEMBER 1
Running Back to You

The preacher asked, "Will you come?" it was time for the altar call. I sat there with sweaty palms and a warm feeling that started near my heart and traveled throughout my body. I felt a pull to get up and go to the altar. This feeling was hard to ignore because I knew it was God calling me. The preacher then pointed at me and said, "You stand up." With tears in my eyes, and a fire burning inside I got up.

I stood there waiting to hear what he had to say. "I don't know what you're going through, but God is telling me whatever you're thinking about doing, DO IT. It's going to be huge. You already have a lot of people doubting you, but God will see you through it." With all my sorrows, hurts, regrets, fears and insecurities, I cried.

I began thanking God, and giving everything over to him on that day. I went to the altar and prayed asking for forgiveness. I cried out until he saved me!

God wants us to live an abundant life, we are not to suppress our hurts, and let it eat away at us. Like the scripture says, we are to confess our faults and learn from them. Find comfort in God and trust he will heal all wounds. We women have been the rock and the epitome of strength for so long. It is now time for us to be transparent about our feelings, and express our hurts, fears, and faults without guilt or shame.

"Peace I leave with you, my peace I give unto you: not as the world giveth, give I unto you. Let not your heart be troubled, neither let it be afraid"
John 14:27

RECLAIM! RECOVER! REGAIN!

*I decided to take back what had been stolen from me throughout the years. I ran to my abusers and took back my **CONFIDENCE**. I reclaimed my **DREAMS** from the nay-sayers. I kicked down the pessimists' door and recovered my **HOPE**. I snatched my **JOY** out of the fire from my trials. I laid my past to rest and regained my **PEACE**. I stood head on with the evil one and demanded my **LIFE** back!*

"You have to fight the fight to prove you're a winner"
-Pastor Winston C. Reeves

YOUR TROUBLES ARE NOT YOUR TROUBLES

Growing up I used to think my problems weren't important enough for God. I would hear preachers talk about how mighty and great He is, but I only thought He could fix BIG problems. I would hear people testify in church about how God blessed them with material things like a new car, job, or house. I never heard anyone talk about being delivered from depression or low self-esteem. So I figured only I could make myself feel better.

I always knew I had a calling to write and motivate others. Unfortunately, my own self-esteem was so low, that every time I would think to do something I'd "think" myself out of it. I even struggled with completing my first book because I didn't feel I was "qualified" enough.

I still remember the day everything "clicked" for me. I was sitting at the table doing a little bible study and I came across the story of Moses. The Lord sent Moses to tell Pharaoh to free the Jews. After he heard this he said, Ex 4:10 "O Lord, I have never been eloquent, neither in the past nor since you have spoken to your servant. I am slow of speech and tongue."

Reading this blew me away. I had no idea men in the bible had issues with low self-esteem and doubt. How deep were his insecurities? He had been given an order straight from God, and yet he still had doubt. Moses' problem was that he was looking at what he could produce instead of what God could produce through Him.

God responded, Ex 4:11 "Who gave man his mouth? Who makes him deaf or mute? Who gives him sight or makes him blind?"

"Is it not I, the Lord? Now go; I will help you speak and will teach you what to say." That day I realized that I could depend on God for everything. He was the answer to all my problems. He completed me in areas I once felt inadequate.

As a young girl I wasn't aware of the vices the devil used to try to destroy and keep me from discovering who I am in Christ. I remember unsuccessfully looking for my confidence in men, jobs, hobbies, strangers and friends. I was tired of being bound by fear and insecurities. After many broken hearts and sleepless nights I turned to God when I had no where else to go.

I've come a long way from being the insecure little girl I wrote about in my journal. God has brought me from rock bottom to heights I never thought I could reach. My pain was real and I thank God everyday that I made it through. In Him I found my everlasting confidence.

My husband walked into the room and asked, "Are you ok? We've been calling you." I'd been so engulfed in reading my journal I didn't hear them calling me. I told him I was ok. "What's that in your hand?" he asked. I looked at him teary eyed and said, "This is going to be the book that gives someone courage to see past their troubles one day."

"This one thing I do, forgetting those things which are behind, and reaching forth unto those things which are before. I press toward the mark for the prize of the high calling of God in Christ Jesus"
Philippians 3:13-14

This Journal Belongs To:

_____

REFLECTIONS

Can you recall a situation that has hurt you in the past? Are you still holding on to the pain?

What things about yourself are you insecure about?

What are you passionate about and what drives you to pursue your dreams?

Is there anything holding you back from pursing your dreams?

If so, what can you do to overcome these obstacles?

_____

_____

_____

_____

_____

_____

_____

_____

_____

_____

_____

_____

_____

_____

_____

_____

_____

_____

_____

_____

_____

_____

_____

_____

_____

_____

_____

QUESTIONS? COMMENTS?

CONTACT ANGELICA

EMAIL:

ANGELICALEIGHW@YAHOO.COM

WEBSITE:

WEDREAMTOO.WORDPRESS.COM

Made in the USA
Columbia, SC
11 July 2018